INHERIT THE BEAUTY WITHIN

POEMS BY KELLY GARNER

ISBN: 978-63795-239-9

EDITOR - WRIGHTINK EDITORAL SERVICES

COVER GRAPHIC DESIGNER - MDM.BRAND

INHERITTHEBEAUTYWITHINBLOG.COM

YOUTUBE - INHER8

INSTAGRAM - @KELLYG_DUHPOEIT

DEDICATION PAGE

This book is dedicated to my sol within. Eye am no longer blinded by my light and see the full spectrum of all my angles. Eye am the architect.

TABLE OF CONTENTS

RHYTHM

APPLE

FEEL GOD

AM I INTO DEEP?

THE ARCHITECTS

SEX IS

UNDER-STAND-INN

GET WELL SOON

THE LEDGE OF KNOWING

I BEAM

IN THE DARKNESS

SCARS VS SAFETY

EVERYTHING IS EVERYTHING

RETRAIN THE BRAIN FROM THINKING THE
SAME

MOTHER, NATURE

CHALLENGE MY ART: ECOSYSTEM (BONUS)*

RHYTHM

This is my canvas, so let me paint,

create any and everything that flows from my head.

Like the rays from the Sun, it does not matter which one

you will still get touched and kissed at least once.

Just like my words, though it may not burn you at first,

but deep in your soul it will have you questioning your worth.

APPLE

He said,

"You so deep I can't breathe".

She said,

"Baby, I am genetically deep and poetically sweet,

like the core of an apple except I am the seed.

Sweet in knowing that the seed can bring new life again,

Deep in knowing the seed can withstand

all that is given from the land.

Deeply rooted and sprouting sweetly.

The seed is the heart and the core of the man

held in the womb-man".

FEEL GOD

I love when I feel good,

if I were a guy

it would probably feel like having a hard wood.

Feeling every sensation,

every penetration of happiness, pure bliss.

I love when I feel good,

like a leaf floating in the wind.

Feeling like it is flying though it has no wings,

but it knows there is no limit because the wings grow within.

I love when I feel good.

AM I IN TOO DEEP?

I tried to swim back to shore,

but the current from the waves decided to keep me out

a little more.

Am I into deep?

I just wanted to sit on the sand and watch the Sunset,

but ended up staying until the Moon slept.

And the many Stars were no help,

for they stayed gazing into my eyes

as I stayed gazing back at them

as if I were staring at myself.

So, then I tried yelling for help,

but the vibration from my voice just seemed to melt,

right into the waves as if they were being stacked on a shelf,

which seemed to help the breeze pick up speed

and ran right into me.

Luckily, I was already off my feet.

Am I into deep?

THE ARCHITECTS

Hey stranger, or shall I say old friend,

old kindred spirit, old remnants of me, how you be?

What is this resemblance that I see?

The resemblance that I feel.

I like how we have been building,

the landscape such an appeal.

Will the full sculpture be revealed?

Will we be the ones finalizing the deal?

SEX IS...

Not looking at my ass because you like the reflection,

but looking in my eyes because you feel the connection.

Creating inner-twining energies that have been manifesting from our thoughts,

creating magnetic rhythm that flows to the beat of our hearts,

that releases vibrational frequencies that our bodies dance to non-stop.

Going deeper, in-depth,

until we both create our own forms of love,

coming together in this moment,

there we sit,

elevating higher,

because sex is also our drug.

Sex is…

Not looking in my eyes because you feel the connection,

but looking at my ass because you like the reflection.

Yet you feeling my vibe cause you grabbing my thighs,

so, baby tell me why you cannot look me in my eyes,

what is it, pride?

I mean, you all up in my insides.

Having given you a piece of me,

I would figure you could see through me,

or even see a piece of me,

But instead,

I just go back and forth with thoughts in my head

asking myself all these questions instead,

there used to be so much that was said,

but now all we do is roll up in bed.

UNDER-STAND-INN

Everybody acts like they care until it gets real,

acting like they know how to deal,

but when it comes to playing their hand, it is too real for them to

understand.

They renig, leaving you, feeling alone.

Stuck, no umbrella in your hand.

Nothing for you to stand under, stand over, stand by, or stand near.

No vision, it is blurry, very unclear.

They are too scared to lose hiding behind "their truth".

What then are you supposed to do?

There is nothing but space it is just a matter of time,

buckle up, come on, and enjoy the ride,

here comes truth looking you dead in the eye.

No windshield wipers needed, no defrost tonight

because we slowly burning off that thing called pride.

Next comes ego,

but just the salty arrogant cocky side.

Now for a dose of Love,

you know that special magical love that is up above.

You know it is everywhere so why chose to love fear?

Everybody acts like they care until it gets real!

Acting like they really know how to truly deal.

But when it comes to playing their hand and shit is just too real for them to understand.

Fear comes in and consumes their hand,

then they renig, and back to the top where we start again.

Everybody acts……

GET WELL SOON

I cry for you in silence because I know that you are still hurting.

I cry for you in silence because I know that you feel broken.

I wish I could heal the wound so the pain can no longer resume.

I wish I could hide the pain so the Sun can come shine from behind the rain.

I hope you regain your mental strength and not feel strained or drained.

Maintaining one's mental is hard work,

staying emotionally balanced is far from a joke,

keeping stabilization in all fields: body, mind, and soul.

You must gain control to feel whole.

Balance the thoughts,

align them with your wants and needs,

see if that will please your soul and make you feel whole,

and if not then try something else.

Keep looking for that feeling that makes you feel free with positivity to balance really being complete.

See that is the catch, you will see.

Keep trying, do not give up.

Find your feeling.

It will lead you to your true love which really is already within and mend the brokenness that wants to extend.

I cry for you in silence, I hope you learn to cope,

some find balance and some won't.

Balance brings peace,

and with no peace you are weak,

which leaves you open for any and everything.

Get well soon.

THE LEDGE OF KNOWING

Commercial for commerce steady getting our mind worked.

Some of us not thinking for ourselves no books on the shelf.

Just waiting on the help when the only help you gone get is from yourself.

Question everything and take no one's word.

Just like the media you are told only what they want you to know,

if you do not check the knowledge for yourself, how will you truly grow?

Go to the "ledge" of "knowing" until all you are left with is the "showing".

Applied Knowledge is Power.

I BEAM

We all have a purpose of being!

Do you like who you are becoming?

Or are you just letting you be? Who are you being?

Are you being what you want to be,

or what you want someone else to see?

It may sound confusing so let me breakdown the "be".

See life is about learning and growing, "be-ing" and "be-coming".

Be-in still,

be-in peace,

be-in love,

be-in free,

be-in harmony;

one with all you see.

"Be-coming" is growing into "be-ing" though sometimes you may
fall.

Be-coming the be-am of stillness, of peace, of love.

Shine like the far away stars from up above,

but really from within because above is just a reflection of your
being,

of your beam, your brightness, your shine;

it is the intellect consciousness of your mind.

Your souls' eye that becomes activated through the spine.

The same symbol used for medicine in the hospitals and the schools.

Don't you see the clues? It is all around you it is up for you to choose.

See me I beam, becoming and being,

because when you breakdown "beam" you get Be and Am.

I Be. I Am.

I beam like the infinite atoms (Adams) that comes from matter

that transcends into all factors.

because that I Am.

Light.

IN THE DARKNESS

Shootin' stars fallin' stars,

we are all stars it does not matter where you are.

We are matter combined into Atoms or Adams…

…who is A-man…Amen.

The nature of a man which got caught up by Satan.

The Moon-Star Eve made him cave-in,

or some would say she helped make him become awaken.

For the snake is really the spine that helps keep the chakras align,

and opens the third eye,

that helps activate the pineal gland inside the man name atom.

Atoms.Adams/MoonStar.Monster

SCARS VS SAFETY

Broken scars afraid to try again.

Do not be afraid, be a friend.

Let the wounds mend and then begin again.

To Love is to Love yourself first.

Ready and willing to share your Love because it feels like you are
going to burst.

Ready to give in, give all the Love you are feeling from within.

You may run into scared little boys acting like men, all pretend.

All a front, forgetting about catching the back end.

When you fall in Love you will feel the pain from all around,

you did not place a safety net to protect any of your steps.

That is why it is best to rise in Love.

Fly high like the winds,

the elevation taking you higher like you are floating off the ground.

Ready to give in,

give all the Love you are feeling from within.

Fly in Love.

Rise in Love.

Healing scars afraid to try again,

get acquainted with afraid and say never again.

Never again will I deny myself of a friend.

Be your own best friend and you will never feel alone again.

Even if you cause your own scars do not give up.

Give the benefit of the doubt

because without a doubt everything always works itself out.

EVERYTHING IS EVERYTHING

I ain't been through nothing but my anceStars have,

beaten and stabbed, hell we still going through that.

Hold up,

let me dig a little deeper and go further back.

I ain't been through nothing but my anceStars have,

taken as slaves, used as camels and calves.

Let me break it down and give you a little math.

See we come from that Universe,

we studied because we the subjects:

Astrology, Astronomy, Chemistry, and Math.

See they don't want U-N-I-2-con-Verse on these things,

they will say, "it's the wrong path,

stick to the 1+1, the basics, you know the math."

But see it is simple and yet so complex.

Once you break it down you will see the hex.

Everything is twisted, turned, inside and out,

front, back, unreasonable doubt.

Zig, zag, up, down.

pick one,

it don't matter

you will still come up with the same results,

because everything is everything.

RETRAIN THE BRAIN FROM THINKING
THE SAME

It is the egotistical,

systematical,

tangible defaults

that can have a person thinking without using their heart.

Let alone the mind,

that is connected to the spine, that keeps the chakras aligned.

But time is an illusion,

this is not a race,

do things at your own pace.

Do not let society throw it in your face.

Balance is key in everything you do,

keep those inner-G's leveled or get consumed.

Consumed by the ego making you think you are free,

though in reality you are nothing but weak.

Balance your thoughts to be aligned with your heart

or shall I say spirit because that is where it starts.

MOTHER, NATURE

Seeing my mother plant flowers in the yard (daisies, and carnations),
from climbing trees, picking plums, and blackberries.
From helping Grandma plant watermelons and squash, peanuts, and
pecans.
Man, the sand between my feet,
or playing in the water at the beach,
Mother Nature I am so glad I have grown to see
the beauty in all that you are.
All you possess.
Because of you, life taste so sweet,
like sweet nectar from a peach.
You and I have grown together endlessly,
resting "inn" complete,
because we are infinite energy,
Forever giving back like water to the sea.
Being what we were created to be.
The same but in different form.
Mirror reflection.
Oh, how I have learned your many lessons.
How you withstand through all four seasons,
tornadoes, hurricanes, earthquakes, and twisters.
Your patience shows your resilience.
The animals cannot wait to be in your love.
The birds sing sweet tunes from up above.
Chemtrails cannot stop you, nor HAARP, or public pollution.
Mother Nature, we know you are part of the solution!

CHALLENGE MY ART: ECOSYSTEM

Today I opened the dictionary and decided the first word I see I will
express upon:

Ecosystem – *n.* (*ecology*)
a system comprising a community of living organisms and its
surroundings.

I am like an ecosystem,
condensing every living thing around me into a simpler form for me
to understand,
in-order for me to inner stand the environment placed in my hands.
Maneuvering towards the best route
making sure my soul is the one leading with no doubts.
Over-standing the reality before me,
trying to connect with every living organism that crosses my path,
adding up the similarities and balancing out the differences that
clash.
Trying to create only sweet memories where I can look back on upon
and laugh.
I am an ever-evolving ecosystem.

(Reference: Webster's Dictionary)

ABOUT THE AUTHOR

Kelly Garner was born and raised on the Sea Islands of Frogmore, commonly known as St. Helena Island on the coasts of South Carolina. She stems from the beautiful triumphant Gullah Geechee (Guale) Tribe, known for their heroism in The Gullah Wars/Seminole Wars/The Invisible Wars (bka The Civil Wars). Kelly is an original Native of the Americas.

Kelly Garner started writing poetry at the age of twelve. Her first poem was imagining she was a bird, and she has been flying ever since. She has a warrior spirit like her anceStars and sees no limits when it comes to her crafts. *Inherit the Beauty Within* is the first self-published book of many to come from the up-and-coming author. She utilizes writing to release her emotions and to create a nu reality as she continues to perfect her craft…

> "Writing brings life to my ideas, it creates new angles for me to shape, and new views for me to relate".

Kelly loves reading books on all subject matters – (hue man) nature being her favorite topic. She also enjoys gardening, trying new things, meeting new people, and spending time with her love ones. Kelly currently resides in Atlanta, Georgia where she has called it her second home for the past eighteen years.

Made in the USA
Columbia, SC
23 May 2022

60780091R00018